Saints

OF THE

ROMAN MISSAL

PRAY FOR US

SAINTS
OF THE
ROMAN MISSAL

PRAY FOR US

J. Michael Thompson

Liguori
LIGUORI, MISSOURI

Imprimi Potest:
Harry Grile, CSsR, Provincial
Denver Province, The Redemptorists

Published by Liguori Publications
Liguori, Missouri 63057

To order, call 800-325-9521, or visit liguori.org.

Library of Congress Cataloging-in-Publication Data

Thompson, J. Michael, 1953-
  Saints of the Roman missal, pray for us / by J. Michael Thompson.—1st ed.
    p. cm.
  ISBN 978-0-7648-2103-5
  1. Christian saints—Biography. 2. Christian saints—Prayers and devotions.
  3. Catholic Church. Missale Romanum (1970) I. Title.
  BX4655.3.T49 2012
  282.092'2—dc23
  [B]
                          2012008367

Music engraving by Michael Silhavy

Hymn texts Copyright © 2010 World Library Publications. Used with permission.

Photo credits—Cover, from left, Canossian Daughters of Charity; St. Joseph's Oratory, Shutterstock; and Fondazione Voce di Padre Pio, Italy; St. Joseph's Oratory, page 12; Canossian Daughters of Charity, 20; Wikipedia, 28, 36, 44, 60, 76, 84, 92, 100, 108, 116; Archdiocese of Guadalajara (Mexico), 52; Ken Jan Woo, 68; Trinity Stores, 124; Shutterstock, 132

Liguori Publications, a nonprofit corporation, is an apostolate of The Redemptorists. To learn more about The Redemptorists, visit Redemptorists.com.

Printed in the United States of America
16 15 14 13 12 / 5 4 3 2 1
First Edition

CONTENTS

FOREWORD

J. Michael Thompson's *Saints of the Roman Missal, Pray for Us* is a timely and needed contribution to liturgical devotion inspired by the lives of the saints. This volume not only provides information for worshipers and homilists about the saints found in the third post-Vatican II edition of the *Missale Romanum*, it offers wonderful hymn texts for those individuals and communities who would choose to honor the saints in song at their feast day celebrations of the *Liturgy of the Hours* and the Eucharist.

The saints honored range from the patristic era—such as Apollinaris of Ravenna and Catherine of Alexandria—to contemporaries André Bessette, Teresa Benedicta of the Cross (Edith Stein), and Pio of Pietrelcina (Padre Pio), and happily represent ethnic communities with the inclusion of Josephine Bakhita and Andrew Dung-Lac, plus Augustine Zhao Rong, who advocated universality for the Church.

Christian hymnody has not always simply blessed or petitioned the triune God or one of the divine persons. Hymns have also recounted the narratives of Christian heroes and heroines, from the Ambrosian lyrics written by Saint Ambrose and others who lauded the martyrs of Milan, Nabor, and Felix, through Anabaptist hymnody that at great length recounted the bravery and suffering of the founding fathers and mothers of their reformation movement.

Hymns inspired by the lives of saints tend to fall into two great categories: texts that praise God for the gift of the saint and ask God to bestow the virtues of the saint on the praying community; and texts that seek the intercession of the saint for particular needs of the Church and/or the world.

The hymn for Teresa Benedicta of the Cross offers an example of the first category, where God is praised not only as the triune God but as the God of Israel. This distinction reflects Saint Teresa's own journey of faith as she embraced her Jewish heritage and came to see it transformed in Christ. In the second category of intercession for particular needs, the hymn for Sharbel Makhluf beautifully evokes his Lebanese and Maronite Catholic heritage while directly petitioning his help for worshipers to develop a contemplative asceticism. The author's long experience in leading Christian-sung worship also shines through in the appealing and familiar hymn tunes he has yoked with his inspiring texts.

May this volume help you deepen your appreciation for the power of Christ's victory manifested in the lives of the saints. May it assist preachers to challenge contemporary Christians to respond to God's grace as wholeheartedly as did these saints who are commemorated. And may it provide all Christians a repertoire and band of models for worship songs praising God and his saints.

FATHER JAN MICHAEL JONCAS
UNIVERSITY OF ST. THOMAS
ST. PAUL, MINNESOTA

INTRODUCTION

On the First Sunday of Advent in 2011, the third edition of *The Roman Missal* began to be prayed in parishes throughout the United States. One of the new components is the content for the Calendar of Saints. *The Roman Missal* published in the United States includes the General Roman Calendar that is used in the Catholic Church throughout the world, as well as the names of certain saints whose observance is remembered only in the United States. The universal nature of the Church is underscored, however, by the inclusion of saints from all over the world, such as Josephine Bakhita of the Sudan, Damien of Hawaii, Augustine Zhao Rong of China, Sharbel Makhluf of Lebanon, Lorenzo (Lawrence) Ruiz of the Philippines, and Andrew Dung-Lac of Vietnam.

Some saints, such as Adalbert, Louis Mary de Monfort, Rita of Cascia, Apollinaris, and Catherine of Alexandria, are being restored to the General Roman Calendar after being removed during a revision of the calendar in 1969. New saints have also been canonized since the last *Roman Missal* was published and are now in the third edition. These include André Bessette, Josephine Bakhita, Damien, Sharbel, Teresa Benedicta of the Cross, and Padre Pio. Finally, new propers or prayers for particular parts of the Mass are included, such as those for Saint Andrew Dung-Lac.

This book invites you to enter into the life and service of each of these sixteen saints and offers you an opportunity to pray with them as you contemplate their witness. An image of each saint, his or her

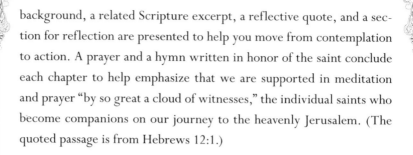

background, a related Scripture excerpt, a reflective quote, and a section for reflection are presented to help you move from contemplation to action. A prayer and a hymn written in honor of the saint conclude each chapter to help emphasize that we are supported in meditation and prayer "by so great a cloud of witnesses," the individual saints who become companions on our journey to the heavenly Jerusalem. (The quoted passage is from Hebrews 12:1.)

Patron of caregivers and those sick

SAINT
ANDRÉ BESSETTE
PRAY FOR US

FEAST
January 6

BORN
August 9, 1845,
Mont-Saint-Grégoire,
Quebec

DIED
January 6, 1937,
Montreal

CANONIZED
October 17, 2010,
by Pope Benedict XVI

Sometimes, the deck seems stacked, but not in one's favor.

Alfred Bessette, the eighth of twelve children in his family, was small of stature and sickly. When he was twelve, both of his parents died. He worked at job after job—farm hand, shoemaker, baker, blacksmith, factory worker—and he failed in all of these trades. In 1870, his pastor sent him to the Holy Cross Brothers in Montreal with a note to the superior that said, "I am sending you a saint." However, the brothers saw only a twenty-five-year-old man who could neither read nor write and lacked skill and physical strength, so they asked him to leave. In desperation, the young man asked the bishop for help. The bishop persuaded the community to try again, and the community took him in. He was given the name André, professed his vows as a new member of the Holy Cross, and was assigned the job of porter at the Notre Dame College, a school for boys ages seven to twelve. André joked, "At the end of my novitiate, my superiors showed me the door— and there I stayed for forty years!"

Brother André's work at the door brought him face to face with many poor and needy people, and he was always eager to pray with and for them. He visited the sick and often anointed them with oil from the lamp that burned in the college chapel. Word spread through the city of his ability to heal. This became more pronounced during an epidemic, when he nursed the sick at a nearby college and one of his patients died. Because of this, he was under suspicion by religious and medical authorities alike, but his response was, "I do not cure. Saint Joseph cures."

His devotion to Saint Joseph, foster father of the Savior, fueled his desire to have the property of Mount Royal topped with a shrine to "good Saint Joseph." The shrine was begun with nickels, dimes, and pennies, and built only as donations increased. As the shrine grew, so did the number of cures; however Brother André did not live to see the

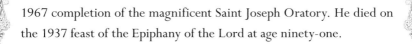

1967 completion of the magnificent Saint Joseph Oratory. He died on the 1937 feast of the Epiphany of the Lord at age ninety-one.

"This is how all will know that you are my disciples, [says the Lord], if you have love for one another."

JOHN 13:35

*"It is with the smallest brushes
that the artist paints the most
exquisitely beautiful pictures."*

SAINT ANDRÉ BESSETTE

FOR REFLECTION

In the life of each Christian comes the chance to do something—some sort of good work or some charitable act. Quite often, the chance is missed because it looks as if we lack the resources to accomplish our desire. The life and service of Saint André Bessette teaches us that the only way to get something done is to *begin*, no matter how small the beginning might be. Begin the work with God's blessing, then persevere, and let God take the beginning and run with it.

PRAYER

O God,
Your word has taught us to not despise the little things.
We thank you for the life and witness of Saint André Bessette,
for whom rejection, illness, and humble tasks
were ways to serve you and give you glory.

May his example of sincere and faithful love and service
to the poor, the sick, and lonely
urge us to do the same as we show our love for you
in the least of these, your Son's brothers and sisters.

We ask this through Christ our Lord.

Amen.

A Hymn for Saint André Bessette

1. In care for poor and sickly folk,
   The Lord has told us well,
   We care for him; in doing so
   Our love for God we tell.

2. Thus André, in his humble life,
   Poor, chaste, obedient man,
   Cared for the poor of Montreal,
   As laid out in God's plan.

3. His love for good Saint Joseph led
   A chapel to be raised,
   And all his work with grace was crowned
   For labors giv'n in praise.

J. MICHAEL THOMPSON
CM, TUNE: "HYFRYDOL" ("JERUSALEM, MY HAPPY HOME")
TEXT COPYRIGHT 2010 WORLD LIBRARY PUBLICATIONS. USED WITH PERMISSION.

A Hymn for Saint André Bessette

HYFRYDOL
CM

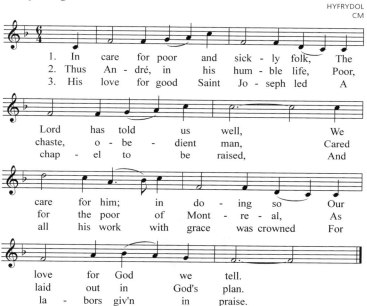

1. In care for poor and sick - ly folk, The
2. Thus An - dré, in his hum - ble life, Poor,
3. His love for good Saint Jo - seph led A

Lord has told us well, We
chaste, o - be - dient man, Cared
chap - el to be raised, And

care for him; in do - ing so Our
for the poor of Mont - re - al, As
all his work with grace was crowned For

love for God we tell.
laid out in God's plan.
la - bors giv'n in praise.

Patron of Sudan and those sexually abused as children

SAINT
JOSEPHINE BAKHITA
PRAY FOR US

FEAST
February 8

BORN
c. 1869,
Olgossa, Darfur, Sudan

DIED
February 8, 1947,
Schio, Veneto, Italy

CANONIZED
October 1, 2000,
by Pope John Paul II

A young woman from what is today South Sudan is stolen from her village by a slave trader and is sold to the Italian consul. This might sound like the beginning of a novel. However, it was a most cruel reality for a girl whom the slave dealers called "Bakhita," which means "fortunate" in her native language.

The experiences of the slave markets in El Obeid and Khartoum, Sudan, were altogether too real and horrifying for this young woman, who was born around 1869. She was sold several times to different owners and lived through enormous humiliation and physical and moral suffering.

In Khartoum, Callisto Legnani, the Italian consul, purchased Bakhita. He took her back to Italy when political strife arose in Sudan. In Italy, Bakhita became the babysitter and friend of his daughter, Mimmina Michieli. When Mr. and Mrs. Michieli went back to Africa, Bakhita and Mimmina were sent to the school of the Canossian Sisters in Venice.

It was in this convent that Bakhita came to know God. She received the sacraments of Christian initiation and was given the name Josephine on January 9, 1890. From then on, she was often seen revering the baptismal font: "Here," said she, "I became a daughter of God!"

When the Michieli family returned, Josephine Bakhita told them she was planning on joining the sisters' community, and because she lived in Italy, she was no longer to be considered a slave or the property of anyone else. On December 8, 1896, she took her vows to the God whom she called "the Master."

Saint Josephine served her community in Schio by cooking, sewing, embroidering, and acting as portress or doorkeeper at the convent. She did this for fifty years, winning the hearts of the children in the schools and community as she consoled the poor and ill and provided encouragement for those who came to the convent for help.

Her last years were troubled by a long, painful illness. However, she remained full of faith and hope despite her ill health. Josephine Bakhita died on February 8, 1947, surrounded by her sisters.

The LORD's acts of mercy are not exhausted,
His compassion is not spent;
They are renewed each morning—
Great is your faithfulness!
The LORD is my portion, I tell myself,
Therefore I will hope in him.

LAMENTATIONS 3:22–24

"Seeing the sun, the moon and the stars,
I said to myself: 'Who could be the Master of these
beautiful things?' And I felt a great desire to see Him,
to know Him, and to pay Him homage...."

SAINT JOSEPHINE BAKHITA

FOR REFLECTION

For many people, the search for freedom to do what one wishes at the time that one wishes is of utmost importance.

One thing that becomes apparent when we reflect on the life of Saint Josephine Bakhita is that true freedom comes from knowing "the Master," the God who is revealed to us in the person of Jesus Christ. Bakhita encouraged those in her community and the poor with whom she came in contact with the words, "Be good, love the Lord, pray for those who do not know him. What a great grace it is to know God!"

In this, she reflects Saint Paul's teaching: "...Now that you have been freed from sin and have become slaves of God, the benefit that you have leads to sanctification, and its end is eternal life" (Romans 6:22).

PRAYER

God of the lowly and the lost,
you led your daughter, Josephine Bakhita,
through the horrors of slavery
to spiritual and physical freedom
as a child of yours in Christ Jesus.

May her example of humble and joyful service
of you and of your people
inspire us to know you, to love you, and to serve you
in all that we do.

May we witness to your love
to all those we encounter.

We ask this through Christ our Lord.

Amen.

A Hymn for Saint Bakhita

1. Jesus left his throne in heaven,
   Humbly coming as a slave,
   Here his love and his obedience
   Were the ransom that still saves:
   Strong the song the Church now raises
   For this humble Virgin's day,
   Praising God that, through all struggles,
   She was led to Christ, the Way.

2. As a child torn from her fam'ly,
   Made a slave, great suff'ring bore,
   And by those who took her childhood,
   Named "Bakhita" evermore.
   Brought to Italy and rescued
   By Canossian sisters there,
   She found Christ and then was baptized,
   Lived in service and in prayer.

3. As the virgins in the Gospel,
   Josephine was filled with light,
   Daily serving at her convent,
   Greeting all with heaven's sight;
   Loving all with Jesus' mercy,
   Treating each as she would him—
   Persevered through pain and sorrow,
   Making life her off'ring hymn.

J. MICHAEL THOMPSON
87 87 D, TUNE: "BEACH SPRING" ("GOD OF DAY AND GOD OF DARKNESS")
TEXT COPYRIGHT 2010 WORLD LIBRARY PUBLICATIONS. USED WITH PERMISSION.

A Hymn for Saint Bakhita

BEACH SPRING
87 87 D

1. Je-sus left his throne in heav - en, Hum - bly
2. As a child torn from her fam - 'ly, Made a
3. As the vir - gins in the Gos - pel, Jo - seph-

com - ing as a slave, Here his
slave, great suf - f'ring bore, And by
ine was filled with light, Dai - ly

love and his o - be - dience Were the
those who took her child - hood, Named "Bak -
serv - ing at her con - vent, Greet - ing

ran - som that still saves: Strong the
hi - ta" ev - er - more. Brought to
all with heav - en's sight; Lov - ing

song the Church now rais - es For the
It - a - ly and res - cued By Can -
all with Je - sus' mer - cy, Treat - ing

hum - ble Vir - gin's day, Prais - ing
os - sian sis - ters there, She found
each as she would him– Per - sev -

God that, through all strug - gles, She was
Christ and then was bap - tized, Lived in
ered through pain and sor - row, Mak - ing

led to Christ, the Way.
ser - vice and in prayer.
life her off - 'ring hymn.

*Patron of Bohemia, Czech Republic,
Poland, Prague, Prussia*

SAINT ADALBERT

PRAY FOR US

FEAST
April 23

BORN
c. 957,
Libice nad Cidlinou,
Bohemia

DIED
Martyred April 23, 997,
Pomerania, Poland

CANONIZED
999

In April 1997, Blessed John Paul II and about a million believers of several different ecclesial communions—including Roman Catholics, Eastern Orthodox, and Protestants—gathered in the city of Gniezno, Poland, to commemorate the 1,000th anniversary of the martyrdom of Saint Adalbert. Who was he, and why was he worth bringing up such a long time after his death?

Adalbert was born in 956, and baptized Vojtech. His parents, Prince Slavnik and Strezislava, were Czech nobles who had six sons. Vojtech studied in Magdeburg in Thuringia with Archbishop Adalbert for ten years, and at his mentor's death in 980, he took the name Adalbert for himself. In that year, he was ordained to the priesthood. Two years later, he was made the bishop of Prague. He set a rigorous regimen of charity, austerity, and devoted service to Church and people. He preached and worked against idolatry, polygamy, and the slave trade.

In 989, he resigned his position as bishop and entered a Benedictine monastery in Rome, where he remained for four years. In 993, Pope John XV sent him back and appointed him bishop of Prague once again. He then founded the first monastery in Czech lands in the town of Brevnov. Great civil strife occurred during his episcopacy, which included the deaths of four of his brothers. Adalbert traveled to Hungary, where he baptized King Geza and his son, Stephen. Then he went to Poland, where he was welcomed by King Boleslaw the Brave. During this time, he entered into missionary work to convert the Prussians.

In the course of this missionary journey, Adalbert tried to cut down one of the oak trees sacred to the local pagan gods and was martyred there in April 997. His body was purchased by King Boleslaw and buried with great honor in the city of Gniezno. He was canonized a few years later and honored by Poles, Czechs, Hungarians, and Germans. The massive bronze doors of the Gniezno Cathedral were created in 1175 and contain eighteen bas-relief sculpted panels that illustrate the life of Saint Adalbert.

Are we beginning to commend ourselves again? Or do we need, as some do, letters of recommendation to you or from you? You are our letter, written on our hearts, known and read by all, shown to be a letter of Christ administered by us, written not in ink but by the Spirit of the living God, not on tablets of stone but on tablets that are hearts of flesh.

2 CORINTHIANS 3:1–3

The mission of the Church, therefore, is fulfilled by
that activity which makes her, obeying the command of
Christ and influenced by the grace and love of the Holy
Spirit, fully present to all men or nations, in order
that, by the example of her life and by her preaching,
by the sacraments and other means of grace, she may
lead them to the faith, the freedom and the peace of
Christ; that thus there may lie open before them a firm
and free road to full participation in
the mystery of Christ.

FROM THE DECREE *AD GENTES*, ON THE MISSIONARY
ACTIVITY OF THE CHURCH, FROM THE SECOND VATICAN
COUNCIL, FROM THE *LITURGY OF THE HOURS*

FOR REFLECTION

The life of Saint Adalbert goes back and forth between success and failure. He did not allow success to go to his head, nor failure to cause him to cease striving to share the Gospel to those who did not know Christ and his love. How often do we encounter opposition in our own lives when we attempt to do God's will and then give up? Saint Adalbert is a good model for us to hear the scriptural admonition from Matthew's Gospel, "Whoever endures to the end will be saved" (Matthew 10:22). God will not let his word be void!

PRAYER

Loving God,
your Son's great commission sent your Church forth
to make disciples of all nations,
baptizing them in the name of the Father, and of the Son,
and of the Holy Spirit,
teaching them to observe all that he had commanded us.

In fidelity to this command,
your servant, the bishop Adalbert,
preached to the peoples of Bohemia, Hungary, Poland, and
the Prussian lands,
and was martyred in witness to your truth.

Inspire in us today a similar desire to spread the Gospel
to those who have not heard it
and to those who have heard it taught with a lack of love and
respect.

We ask this through Christ our Lord.

Amen.

A Hymn for Saint Adalbert

1. Paschal peace and paschal joy
   Bathe our souls with gladness!
   Adalbert, God's shepherd good,
   Leads us out from sadness
   Into pastures safe and sure,
   Christ's own flock now tending.
   From his place in heaven's joy,
   His true guidance sending!

2. Bishop of the Church of Prague,
   Magyars' faithful teacher;
   In the Poles' and Prussians' lands
   Faithful, fervent preacher:
   "Now salvation's day is come!
   Now, the time appointed!
   Come, be baptized; know the Lord!
   Be by him anointed!"

3. Father, Son, and Spirit blest,
   One-in-Three we name you:
   Source of love and light and peace
   We shall ever claim you!
   With your bishop martyr brave
   And the churches founded
   Through your grace and through his work,
   Is your Gospel grounded.

J. MICHAEL THOMPSON
76. 76. D, TUNE: "SAINT KEVIN" ("COME, YE FAITHFUL, RAISE THE STRAIN")
TEXT COPYRIGHT 2010 WORLD LIBRARY PUBLICATIONS. USED WITH PERMISSION.

A Hymn for Saint Adalbert

SAINT KEVIN
76.76.D

1. Pas - chal peace and pas - chal joy
2. Bish - op of the Church of Prague,
3. Fath - er, Son and Spir - it blest,

Bathe our souls with glad - ness!
Mag - yars' faith - ful teach - er;
One - in - Three we name you:

Ad - al - bert, God's shep - herd good,
In the Poles' and Prus - sians' lands
Source of love and light and peace

Leads us out from sad - ness
Faith - ful, fer - vent preach - er:
We shall ev - er claim you!

In - to pas - tures safe and sure,
"Now - sal - va - tion's day is come!
With your bish - op mar - tyr brave

Christ's own flock now tend - ing.
Now, the time ap - point - ed!
And the church - es found - ed

From his place in heav - en's joy,
Come, be bap - tized; know the Lord!
Through your grace and through his work,

His true guid - ance send - ing!
Be by him an - oint - ed!"
Is your Gos - pel ground - ed.

Patron of the Legion of Mary

SAINT LOUIS MARY DE MONFORT

PRAY FOR US

FEAST
April 28

BORN
January 31, 1673,
Montfort, France

DIED
April 28, 1716,
Saint Laurent sur Sèvre,
France

CANONIZED
July 20, 1947,
by Pope Pius XII

It is said that Saint Louis Mary de Monfort's whole life was known for constant prayer, love of the poor, poverty, joy in humiliation, and persecution, yet he emerged as a man of profound holiness.

Louis was born in France in 1673. His family name was Grignion; "de Monfort" indicated the town where he grew up. He was pious as a young child and attended school, university, and seminary. When he was nineteen, he left to study in Paris. On that journey, he gave away all his money to the poor and exchanged his clothing for theirs. At that time, he made a vow to live only on the alms and offerings that he received. He was ordained a priest at the age of twenty-seven, and when he was thirty-two, he found his true vocation: preaching to God's people. He was a talented preacher. His language was down-to-earth, but his presentation was full of fervor and God's love.

His relationships with local bishops were rocky, and since only a bishop could give authority to a priest to preach in his diocese, Louis went to Rome and met with Pope Clement XI to discuss his passion for preaching. The pope sent him back to France with the title "apostolic missionary." This permitted him to preach anywhere.

His fame as a preacher grew to where he founded a community of women—the Daughters of Wisdom and a community of preaching priests, the Company of Mary—to join him in his work. He wrote many books about the Blessed Virgin Mary, which influenced many popes, in particular Popes Leo XIII, Saint Pius X, Pius XII, and Blessed John Paul II. He was devoted and zealous to his call and preached for sixteen years before his body wore out. His last sermon was on "the Tenderness of Jesus and the Incarnate Wisdom of the Father." He died on April 28, 1716.

*For the foolishness of God is wiser than human wisdom,
and the weakness of God is stronger than human strength.*

1 CORINTHIANS 1:25

*"If we do not risk anything for God,
we will never do anything great for him."*

SAINT LOUIS MARY DE MONFORT

FOR REFLECTION

One of the major obstacles in the life of Saint Louis Mary de Monfort was the attitude of a group of Catholics called the Jansenists, who insisted that the average person was unworthy to receive Communion regularly and emphasized the vast gap between God and humanity. Luckily, their teachings were condemned by the Church, but it is still easy to dwell on our unworthiness in the face of our Creator. How often do people today forget that there is any gap whatsoever between the Creator and the creation? May Saint Louis' words and example remind us of the immense love that God has for each of us. This love was exemplified for all times in the coming of the second person of the Trinity to be one of us, to be our brother and our Redeemer. May God be praised!

PRAYER

God of infinite love,
you called your servant Louis Mary de Monfort
to preach to a world grown cold and indifferent
of your Son Jesus Christ, who loved all humanity.

May we risk everything for you,
so that we may do all manner of great things for you
who lives and reigns with your Son and the Holy Spirit,
one God, through endless ages.

Amen.

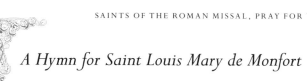

A Hymn for Saint Louis Mary de Monfort

1. The cross is the message that leads to salvation,
   So full of the grace and the power of God!
   This message is foolish for all who cannot heed it,
   But life to those whose feet on its pathway have trod.

2. Saint Louis, your servant, was fervent in preaching,
   He called men and women to work by his side
   In care for the poor and for preaching your salvation;
   His writings and his works declared Christ far and wide.

3. O Trinity blessed, our God from all ages,
   O Father and Spirit and Son, Three-in-One,
   As Louis proclaimed you, so may we ever praise you,
   In all we do and say may your will e'er be done!

J. MICHAEL THOMPSON
TUNE: "WE GATHER TOGETHER"
TEXT COPYRIGHT 2010 WORLD LIBRARY PUBLICATIONS. USED WITH PERMISSION.

A Hymn for Saint Louis Mary de Monfort

WE GATHER TOGETHER
IRREGULAR KREMSER

1. The cross is the mes - sage that
2. Saint Lou - is, your serv - ant, was
3. O Trin - i - ty bless - ed, our

leads to sal - va - tion, So full of the
fer - vent in preach - ing, He called men and
God from all a - ges, O Fath - er and

grace and the pow - er of God! This
wom - en to work by his side In
Spir - it and Son, Three - in - One, As

mes - sage is fool - ish for all who can - not
care for the poor and for preach - ing your sal -
Lou - is pro - claimed you, so may we ev - er

heed it, But life to those whose
va - tion; His writ - ings and his
praise you, In all we do and

feet on its path - way have trod.
works de - clared Christ far and wide.
say may your will e'er be done.

Patron of people suffering from AIDS
and Hansen's Disease

SAINT
DAMIEN OF MOLOKAI
PRAY FOR US

FEAST
May 10

BORN
January 3, 1840,
Tremelo, Belgium

DIED
April 15, 1889,
Molokai, Hawaii

CANONIZED
October 11, 2009,
by Pope Benedict XVI

God's calling is strong.

Joseph de Veuster was born on January 3, 1840, in the Flemish town of Tremelo in Belgium. He was the seventh of eight children. His father was a farmer who expected his big, strong son to take over the family business. However, Joseph felt another calling. Two of his older sisters had become Ursuline nuns, and his brother, Auguste, had joined the Pipcus Fathers, Roman Catholic priests who were members of the Congregation of the Sacred Hearts of Jesus and Mary. At age eighteen, Joseph followed his brother into the same religious community and took the name "Damien," one of the early Roman "unmercenary physicians." Damien's brother was supposed to join a group of religious being sent to a mission in Hawaii. However, he fell ill at the last minute, so Damien volunteered to take his brother's place. Damien's offer to serve was accepted, and in 1864 he arrived in the kingdom of Hawaii. He was not yet a priest but was ordained in May of that year.

Father Damien spent almost ten years on the island of Hawaii in parish work, learning the native language, building churches, and bringing the Good News of the Gospel to the area. In 1873, he responded to a request by his bishop, who was also a member of his religious community, to minister to a colony of men, women, and children with Hansen's Disease, often known as leprosy, who were exiled to the island of Molokai. Molokai was in disrepair and under no form of government supervision. Once on the island, Father Damien became not only the pastor but the doctor, the engineer, the farm supervisor, and even the coffin maker. For the next sixteen years, he labored with his beloved flock. It was not until nearly the end of his life that he actually received additional help, when the Sisters of Saint Francis joined him in his work. Saint Damien contracted Hansen's Disease and died on April 15, 1889.

For I was hungry and you gave me food, I was thirsty and you gave me drink, a stranger and you welcomed me, naked and you clothed me, ill and you cared for me....

Amen, I say to you, what you did not do for one of these least ones, you did not do for me.

MATTHEW 25:35–36, 45

*"Here I am in the midst of my dear lepers. They are
so frightful to see, it is true, but they...have souls
redeemed at the price of the precious blood of our
Divine Savior. He also in his divine charity consoled
lepers. If I cannot cure them as he did, at least I can
console them...."*

FROM A LETTER FROM SAINT DAMIEN
TO THE SUPERIOR GENERAL OF THE PIPCUS FATHERS,
AUGUST 1873, FROM *LITURGY OF THE HOURS*

FOR REFLECTION

One of the true challenges of being a follower of Christ is the requirement to "walk one's talk." As Saint John's First Letter tells us, "Whoever does not love remains in death....Children, let us love not in word or speech but in deed and truth." (1 John 3:14b, 18) Saint Damien's life and death are a call for us to look at the people around us and see their needs so that we might love "in deed and truth."

PRAYER

God of the outcast and the incurable,
you sent your Son, the Good Physician, into this world
to call every person into your loving embrace.
We thank you for the work of men and women
who serve you by caring for the sick and homeless,
and especially for your servant Saint Damien of Molokai.

May his love for you,
shown forth in his care for the lepers of Hawaii,
be an encouragement to us
as we encounter those who are scorned and set aside,
helping us to treat each one as we would treat you.

We ask this through Jesus Christ, your Son, our Lord,
who lives and reigns with you and the Holy Spirit,
one God, forever and ever.

Amen.

A Hymn for Saint Damien of Molokai

1. Christ our Lord, you modeled service,
   Gladly washing others' feet,
   Leading on so all might follow
   In your love so bold and sweet.
   On this day we sing in gladness
   Of a man who left his land,
   Giving all in selfless service,
   Guided by your strong right hand.

2. Damien came to Hawaii
   To proclaim the Gospel's grace:
   Then, when summoned by his bishop,
   Went off to the far, sad place
   Where the lepers of that country
   Had been exiled due to fears.
   Fearless in the face of illness,
   He brought joy amid their tears.

3. Preaching, teaching, building housing,
   Caring for the lepers' pain,
   Following the Good Physician,
   Damien brought hope again
   To the Molokai encampment
   With the means of grace and light;
   Being poor, as was his Master,
   He brought strength in place of fright.

J. MICHAEL THOMPSON
87 87 D, TUNE: "BEACH SPRING" ("GOD OF DAY AND GOD OF DARKNESS")
TEXT COPYRIGHT 2010 WORLD LIBRARY PUBLICATIONS. USED WITH PERMISSION.

A Hymn for Saint Damien of Molokai

BEACH SPRING
87 87 D

1. Christ our Lord, you mod-eled ser - vice, Glad-ly wash - ing oth - ers' feet, Lead-ing on so all might fol - low In your love so bold and sweet. On this day we sing in glad - ness Of a man who left his land, Giv - ing all in self - less ser - vice, Guid-ed by your strong right hand.

2. Da - mi - en came to Ha - wai - i To pro-claim the Gos-pel's grace: Then, when sum - moned by his bish - op, Went off to the far, sad place Where the lep - ers of that coun - try Had been ex - iled due to fears. Fear - less in the face of ill - ness, He brought joy a - mid their tears.

3. Preach-ing, teach - ing, build-ing hous - ing, Car - ing for the lep - ers' pain, Fol - low - ing the Good Phy - si - cian, Da - mi - en brought hope a - gain To the Mo - lo - kai en - camp - ment With the means of grace and light; Be - ing poor, as was his Mas - ter, He brought strength in place of fright.

Patron of Catholic action

SAINT CHRISTOPHER MAGALLANES & COMPANIONS

PRAY FOR US

FEAST
May 21

BORN
July 30, 1869,
Totatiche, Mexico

DIED
May 25, 1927,
Jalisco, Mexico

CANONIZED
May 21, 2000,
by Pope John Paul II

If most of us in the United States were asked to describe the Church of Mexico, one of the first descriptors would probably be "a very Catholic country." Few remember the "time of troubles" when the government of Mexico declared war on the Catholic Church in the 1920s.

Cristóbal (Christopher) Magallanes was born in 1869 to a devout Catholic family of poor farmers. He worked as a shepherd until he entered the seminary at the age of nineteen. His studies completed, he was ordained to the priesthood at age thirty and devoted much of his energies to the evangelization and conversion of the indigenous Huichol tribe.

During the anti-Catholic persecution of the 1920s, when seminaries were closed and all foreign clergy were forced to flee the country, Cristóbal built a seminary in Totatiche. When the government closed it, he opened another, and still another. His seminarians were at the last forced to learn in the homes of the faithful rather than in an institution. Cristóbal did not rise up in revolt. Rather, he wrote and preached against armed rebellion. In the end, he was falsely accused of aiding the Cristeros guerillas. He was arrested in May 1927 and shot to death a few days later, without a trial. He and the twenty-two priests and three laymen who are remembered with him on May 21 were martyred in much the same way.

[Jesus said to his disciples:] "Amen, amen, I say to you, unless a grain of wheat falls to the ground and dies, it remains just a grain of wheat; but if it dies, it produces much fruit....Whoever serves me must follow me, and where I am, there also will my servant be. The Father will honor whoever serves me."

JOHN 12:24–26

"I am innocent and I die innocent.
I forgive with all my heart those responsible for my
death, and I ask God that the shedding of my blood
serve the peace of our divided Mexico!"

CRISTÓBAL (CHRISTOPHER) MAGALLANES

FOR REFLECTION

It is very hard for us to imagine religious persecution in the United States. But in many ways, subtle and not-so-subtle, we are called to give daily witness to the faith we hold within us. When we are tempted to put our faith under the bushel basket, let us be strengthened by the courage of Saint Christopher and his companions so that its light shines forth for all to see it and give glory to our Father in heaven.

PRAYER

God of strength and courage,
you called your priest, Christopher Magallanes, and his
    companions
to witness your presence in their lives
by the unwavering living of their faith in times of turmoil,
even to the giving up of their lives for you and your Church.

In the spirit of your Son's words on the cross,
they forgave those who persecuted and killed them.

Give us the fortitude to witness to your Gospel,
in season and out of season,
and to cling to your cross as the true weapon of victory.

We ask this through Christ our risen Lord.

Amen.

A Hymn for Saint Christopher Magallanes & Companions

1. As the vision came from heaven,
   There was seen a host in white.
   Those of ev'ry land and kindred,
   Standing round the Throne of Light.
   "These, the ones who fought and struggled;
   Grace has brought them through their fears.
   Now the Lamb who suffered leads them;
   God has wiped away their tears."

2. In a time of persecution
   When the Church in Mexico
   Suffered in the fiercest manner
   And the streets with blood did flow,
   God called men and women martyrs
   That their lives in sacrifice
   Might be freely, fully given
   For their faith beyond all price.

3. Christopher and his companions
   Sought to keep the Church alive;
   Teaching, preaching, healing, guiding,
   They did all, in secret, strive.
   When discovered and imprisoned,
   He called out, forgiving all,
   Asking God that his blood's shedding
   Might cause peace from heav'n to fall.

J. MICHAEL THOMPSON
87 87 D, TUNE: "A HYMN TO JOY"
TEXT COPYRIGHT 2010 WORLD LIBRARY PUBLICATIONS. USED WITH PERMISSION.

A Hymn for Saint Christopher Magallanes & Companions

A HYMN TO JOY
87 87 D

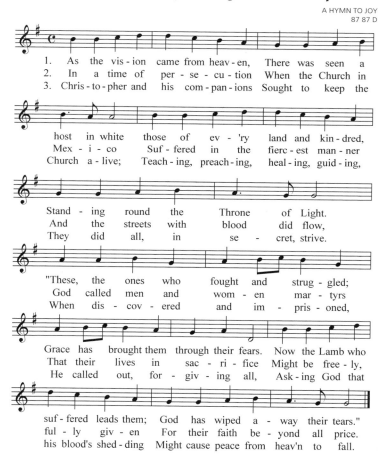

1. As the vis-ion came from heav-en, There was seen a
2. In a time of per-se-cu-tion When the Church in
3. Chris-to-pher and his com-pan-ions Sought to keep the

host in white those of ev-'ry land and kin-dred,
Mex-i-co Suf-fered in the fierc-est man-ner
Church a-live; Teach-ing, preach-ing, heal-ing, guid-ing,

Stand-ing round the Throne of Light.
And the streets with blood did flow,
They did all, in se-cret, strive.

"These, the ones who fought and strug-gled;
God called men and wom-en mar-tyrs
When dis-cov-ered and im-pris-oned,

Grace has brought them through their fears. Now the Lamb who
That their lives in sac-ri-fice Might be free-ly,
He called out, for-giv-ing all, Ask-ing God that

suf-fered leads them; God has wiped a-way their tears."
ful-ly giv-en For their faith be-yond all price.
his blood's shed-ding Might cause peace from heav'n to fall.

Patron of abuse victims,
impossible causes, marriage difficulties

SAINT
RITA OF CASCIA
PRAY FOR US

FEAST
May 22

BORN
1386,
Roccaparena,
Umbria, Italy

DIED
May 22, 1457,
Cascia, Italy

CANONIZED
May 24, 1900,
by Pope Leo XIII

Peace on earth? Maybe. Peace in the family? Especially in a family with serious feuds? That would be much more miraculous, some people would reply with a cynical laugh. But that's why Saint Rita of Cascia is referred to as the "saint of the impossible."

R ita was born in the Umbrian region of Italy in 1386. She married Paolo Mancini when she was only twelve. It was an arranged marriage that her parents insisted upon, despite Rita's pleas to enter a convent. From the beginning, the marriage was torture. Rita's husband was immature, angry, immoral, and had many enemies. Rita responded with prayer and fasting, living a life exemplified by patience, kindness, and humility. Her behavior and example turned her husband from his sinful ways to a life of the Gospel virtue. The couple had two sons, who grew up in a Christ-centered and loving home.

Life changed radically for Rita when her husband was killed in a vendetta by some of his former allies. She struggled to keep her sons faithful to God but was afraid that they would succumb to the ever-present desire for revenge. She turned to the Lord, who took both of them home at an early age.

After the deaths in her family, Rita wanted to enter the Augustinian monastery of Saint Mary Magdalene in the city of Cascia but was repeatedly turned away because the sisters feared being associated with her, due to the bad feelings surrounding the death of her husband. Before they would admit her to the community, she was told she had to reconcile the conflicts that were still blazing between the two families involved in the vendetta. By the time she was thirty-six, she had, with the grace of God, resolved the dispute with the feuding families and was allowed to enter the monastery. She spent the rest of her life there, faithful to the rule of Saint Augustine, and died in 1457.

Rejoice in the Lord always! I shall say it again: rejoice! Your kindness should be known to all. The Lord is near. Have no anxiety at all, but in everything, by prayer and petition, with thanksgiving, make your requests known to God. Then the peace of God that surpasses all understanding will guard your hearts and minds in Christ Jesus.

PHILIPPIANS 4:4–7

If the object of love is what is good,
Then the soul should take its delight in
the higher good, the things of heaven....To help us
to achieve all this, we have the help of the mediator
between God and man. Through him, we shall obtain
all this the more quickly.

FROM A HOMILY ON THE GOSPELS
BY SAINT GREGORY THE GREAT, A POPE,
TAKEN FROM *LITURGY OF THE HOURS*

FOR REFLECTION

S aint Paul said, "We hold this treasure in earthen vessels, that the surpassing power may be of God and not from us" (2 Corinthians 4:7). All our efforts, as were those of Saint Rita, need to be focused on the grace of God and not on our own individual skills. When we recognize that God's will, not ours, is the guiding force, then we will see God's hand and give glory, not to ourselves, but to God through Jesus Christ.

PRAYER

O loving God,
we are taught in your word
that with you all things are possible.
Clinging to this promise,
your servant Rita of Cascia served you faithfully
as daughter, wife, mother, and nun,
seeking always to follow you in humility, obedience, and
      patience.
Through her intercession and by following her example,
help us to always believe
that your love is more powerful than hatred,
and that your peace is stronger than any quarrel.
We ask this through Christ our Lord.

Amen.

A Hymn for Saint Rita of Cascia

1. "Do good to those who hate you;
   Bless all of those who curse;
   Pray hard for those who hurt you
   In all things, bad and worse—
   Show love to all your foemen
   That your reward be great;
   For God's o'erflowing mercies
   Will come and not be late!"

2. When in the life of Rita
   Came murder, hate, and spite,
   She turned her heart to Jesus,
   Her model and delight.
   Instead of seeking vengeance
   She fostered works of grace
   That turned away vendettas
   In light of Jesus' face.

3. For forty years thereafter,
   In service and in prayer
   She lived in peace and concord
   With people everywhere.
   Give glory to the Father,
   The Spirit and the Son,
   Our God, in Triune persons,
   Our God, alone and One.

J. MICHAEL THOMPSON
76 76 D, TUNE: "AURELIA" ("THE CHURCH'S ONE FOUNDATION")
TEXT COPYRIGHT 2010 WORLD LIBRARY PUBLICATIONS. USED WITH PERMISSION.

A Hymn for Saint Rita of Cascia

AURELIA
76 76 D

1. "Do good to those who hate you; Bless all of those who curse; Pray hard for those who hurt you In all things, bad and worse— Show love to all your foe - men That your re - ward be great; For God's o'er - flow - ing mer - cies Will come and not be late!"

2. When in the life of Ri - ta Came mur - der, hate, and spite, She turned her heart to Je - sus, Her mod - el and de - light. In - stead of seek - ing ven - geance She fos - tered works of grace That turned a - way ven - det - tas In light of Je - sus' face.

3. For for - ty years there - af - ter, In ser - vice and in prayer She lived in peace and con - cord With peo - ple ev - ery - where. Give glo - ry to the Fath - er, The Spir - it and the Son, Our God, in Tri - une per - sons, Our God, a - lone and One.

Patron of parish priests of China

SAINT AUGUSTINE ZHAO RONG & COMPANIONS
PRAY FOR US

FEAST

July 9

BORN

1746,

China

DIED

Martyred 1815

119 companions martyred, 1648–1930,

China

CANONIZED

October 1, 2000,

by Pope John Paul II

Tertullian wrote that "the blood of the martyrs is the seed of the Church. Saint Augustine Zhao Rong was won to Christ when, as a soldier, he accompanied Bishop John Gabriel Taurin Dufresse to his execution and witnessed his sufferings and death. After his conversion to Christianity, Augustine went to the local missionaries and expressed his desire to become baptized. He joined the Church and gave his life up to Christ first as a catechist, then as a student for the priesthood, and finally as a diocesan priest. He crowned a faithful life as a missionary priest by giving his life for Christ and his Church in 1815.

As with several other groups of martyred saints from Asia, Saint Augustine Zhao Rong is only the first of many from his 119 companions—bishops, priests, religious, and lay people—who were martyred between 1648 and 1930 in China, ranging in age from nine to seventy-two. Blessed Pope John Paul II beatified them in groups at varying times, and they were canonized together on October 1, 2000, on the feast of Saint Thérèse of Lisieux, the "Little Flower" and patron of all missionaries.

Then one of the elders spoke up and said to me, "Who are these wearing white robes, and where did they come from?" I said to him, "My lord, you are the one who knows." He said to me, "These are the ones who have survived the time of great distress; they have washed their robes and made them white in the blood of the Lamb."

REVELATION 7:13–14

*As the torturers cut off the arm of
the eighteen-year-old altar boy Chi Zhuzi,
he shouted: "Every piece of my flesh, every drop of my
blood will tell you that I am a Christian!"*

FOR REFLECTION

In John's First Letter we are told, "...Whoever is begotten of God conquers the world. And the victory that conquers the world is our faith" (1 John 5:4). When we celebrate the feasts of martyrs, we are not only giving thanks for their witness, we are holding up a mirror before our own lives. The martyrs were faithful in their proclamation of Jesus Christ and gave everything up in order to remain faithful to the Gospel. How does our daily life proclaim this Gospel, especially at times and in places where it might not be convenient to do so?

PRAYER

O God,
from the earliest days of the Church,
your martyrs have witnessed you
by their lives and by their deaths
as their fervor for the Good News of Jesus
enkindled the hearts of your servants.

Saint Augustine Zhao Rong and his companions,
the martyrs of China,
embraced the faith and they gave their lives for you.
They showed the people of their native land.
Keep us ever mindful of their heroic witness
and the need to pray for those who are persecuted yet today.
We ask this through Christ our Lord.

Amen.

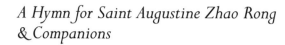

A Hymn for Saint Augustine Zhao Rong & Companions

1. Hear the joyful song celestial,
   Where the martyrs raise their song,
   Praising Christ, the Lord of Heaven,
   Whose free grace has made them strong.
   In the infant Church of China,
   Called by gospel voices bold,
   Saint Augustine and companions
   Died that Christ's truth might be told.

2. In the days when persecution,
   Fueled by fear of foreign ways,
   Sought to stifle Christian teaching
   That had brightened many days,
   One young martyr cried in fervor,
   "Heaven's door is opened wide
   For each one to enter freely!"
   So, for love of Christ, she died.

3. Still their love for Christ and neighbor
   Sheds rich light upon their land,
   Calling forth their sons and daughters
   That in faith they take their stand.
   As they witnessed to the kingdom
   So may our lives testify
   To the freedom and the glory
   Even death cannot defy!

J. MICHAEL THOMPSON
87 87 D , TUNE: "IN BABILONE" ("THERE'S A WIDENESS IN GOD'S MERCY")
TEXT COPYRIGHT 2010 WORLD LIBRARY PUBLICATIONS. USED WITH PERMISSION.

A Hymn for Saint Augustine Zhao Rong & Companions

IN BABILONE
87 87 D

1. Hear the joy - ful song cel - es - tial,
2. In the days when per - se - cu - tion,
3. Still their love for Christ and neigh - bor

Where the mar - tyrs raise their song,
Fueled by fear of for - eign ways,
Sheds rich light up - on their land,

Prais - ing Christ, the Lord of Heav - en
Sought to sti - fle Christ - ian teach - ing
Call - ing forth their sons and daugh - ters

Whose free grace has made them strong.
That had bright - ened man - y days,
That in faith they take their stand.

In the in - fant Church of Chi - na,
One young mar - tyr cried in fer - vor,
As they wit - nessed to the king - dom

Called by gos - pel voic - es bold,
"Heav - en's door is o - pened wide
So may our lives tes - ti - fy

Saint Aug - us - tine and com - pan - ions
For each one to en - ter free - ly!"
To the free - dom and the glo - ry

Died that Christ's truth might be told.
So, for love of Christ, she died,
Ev - en death can - not de - fy!

TEXT COPYRIGHT 2010 WORLD LIBRARY PUBLICATIONS. USED WITH PERMISSION.

Patron of Ravenna

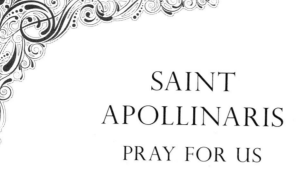

SAINT APOLLINARIS

PRAY FOR US

FEAST

July 23

BORN

Antioch, Turkey

DIED

Martyred c. 79,
Ravenna, Italy

CANONIZED

Before the official process began

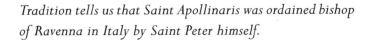

Tradition tells us that Saint Apollinaris was ordained bishop of Ravenna in Italy by Saint Peter himself.

Apollinaris' spreading of the Gospel was so successful that he incurred the wrath of local pagan priests, who beat him almost to death and left him near the seashore to die. He was exiled several times from his home city, but he kept returning to his people, no matter how serious the persecution he encountered. He led the Church of Ravenna for twenty-six years before he was martyred in the name of Jesus Christ

Thus says the LORD God: Look! I myself will search for my sheep and examine them. As a shepherd examines his flock while he himself is among his scattered sheep, so will I examine my sheep. I will deliver them from every place where they were scattered on the day of dark clouds.

EZEKIEL 34:11–12

The Lord of Heaven directed the mind and tongue of the martyrs; through them he overcame the devil on earth and crowned them as martyrs in heaven. Blessed are they who have drunk of this cup!....And so, my dear ones, consider: Although you cannot see with your eyes, do so with your mind and soul, and see that "the death of the saints is precious in the sight of the Lord."

(SERMON 329, "*IN NATALI MARTYRUM*," SAINT AUGUSTINE,
FROM *LITURGY OF THE HOURS*)

FOR REFLECTION

Saint Apollinaris had the gift of healing the sick. This caused many pagans to distrust him as a sorcerer rather than acclaim him as a servant of the living God. How do we cast aspersions on those who can do amazing things simply because those very things are beyond our capacity?

PRAYER

Father of our Lord Jesus Christ,
you provide bishops from your people
who tend your flock with tender care.

As we give thanks to you this day
for the life of your bishop Apollinaris
and for his witness even unto death,
strengthen us in the tasks of our daily affairs
that we may give witness to Christ
both in the things we do and the words we say.

May your Holy Spirit guide us in the way of truth,
and help us bear witness to the love revealed to the world
in the shepherd and guardian of our souls, Jesus Christ,
who lives and reigns with you, O Father,
in the unity of the same Spirit,
one God, for endless ages of ages.

Amen.

A Hymn for Saint Apollinaris

1. As shepherds tend their scattered flock
   To rescue sheep from harm and foe,
   Apollinaris was made bold
   With gospel strength in ev'ry woe.

2. Sent to Ravenna's infant church,
   Made bishop by St. Peter's hand,
   He brought the word and sacraments
   Obedient to his Lord's command.

3. As channel of God's healing pow'r
   He cured the sick and made them whole.
   Imprisonment and exile's fate
   Led him to death, the martyr's goal.

J. MICHAEL THOMPSON
LM, TUNE: *JESU DULCIS MEMORIA* ("O GRACIOUS LIGHT, O SUN DIVINE")

A Hymn for Saint Apollinaris

JESU DULCIS MEMORIA
LM

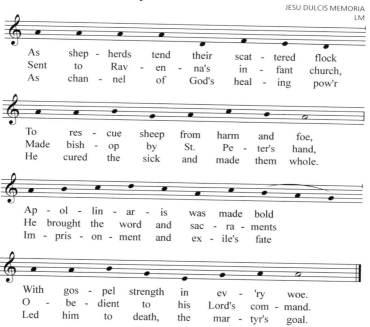

As shep - herds tend their scat - tered flock
Sent to Rav - en - na's in - fant church,
As chan - nel of God's heal - ing pow'r

To res - cue sheep from harm and foe,
Made bish - op by St. Pe - ter's hand,
He cured the sick and made them whole.

Ap - ol - lin - ar - is was made bold
He brought the word and sac - ra - ments
Im - pris - on - ment and ex - ile's fate

With gos - pel strength in ev - 'ry woe.
O - be - dient to his Lord's com - mand.
Led him to death, the mar - tyr's goal.

TEXT COPYRIGHT 2010 WORLD LIBRARY PUBLICATIONS. USED WITH PERMISSION.

83

Secondary patron of Lebanon

SAINT
SHARBEL MAKHLUF
PRAY FOR US

FEAST

July 24

BORN

May 8, 1828,
Bekaa Kafra, North Lebanon

DIED

December 24, 1898

CANONIZED

October 9, 1977,
by Pope Paul VI

Twenty-two different Churches are in communion with the Church of Rome. Saint Sharbel Makhluf was a member of the Maronite Catholic Church. Maronite Catholics pray in the Eastern liturgical style of liturgy but are all still one with the pope of Rome, so we are part of the one Church together.

Joseph Makhluf was born in Turkish-occupied Lebanon in 1828 to a devout peasant family. His father died when he was very young, and he was raised by his uncle, a mule driver. At twenty-three, he went to the monastery and was professed; he was ordained a priest in 1859.

Saint Makhluf spent seven years as an exemplary monk in the monastery and then was permitted to follow the ancient Eastern custom of becoming a "solitary" for twenty-three years in the mountains of Lebanon. His great devotions were to the holy Eucharist and to the *Theotokos*. He died in church on Christmas Eve 1898, when he was seventy years old.

His tomb became a major pilgrimage site in Lebanon, where his body was found to be almost lifelike as late as 1952.

My son, conduct your affairs with humility,
and you will be loved more than a giver of gifts.
Humble yourself the more, the greater you are,
and you will find mercy in the sight of God.

SIRACH 3:17–18

When he beatified Sharbel, Pope Paul VI said of him, "May he make us understand, in a world largely fascinated by wealth and comfort, the paramount value of poverty, penance, and asceticism, to liberate the soul in its ascent to God...."

FOR REFLECTION

The presence of Saint Sharbel Makhluf on the General Roman Calendar of saints helps us to remember that both Eastern and Western styles of liturgical prayer are part of the Catholic Church. In the words of Blessed John Paul II, may Saint Sharbel be a witness to all of us of the necessity of "breathing with both our lungs—the Eastern one as well as the Western one."

PRAYER

O loving God,
you brought Saint Sharbel Makhluf
from the life of a monk in community
to that of a hermit, living on your holy mountain.
May his love for the Blessed Eucharist
teach us to hunger for you, the Bread of Life.

May his confidence in the *Theotokos*, the Mother of your Son,
form us to trust in you without reservation, as she did.
May we set aside the things of earth for the things of heaven,
Where you, O Father, live and reign with your Son and the
    Holy Spirit,
One God, for endless ages of ages.

Amen.

A Hymn for Saint Sharbel Makhluf

1. The mountain heights of Lebanon
   Resound with songs of joy;
   The cedars of that ancient land
   Stand tall as we employ
   Our hymns of praise and thankfulness
   For Sharbel's saintly ways,
   Lived out in strict humility
   That guided all his days.

2. This monk and hermit of the hills,
   Saint Maron's modest son
   Scorned wealth and comfort in his life
   That heaven's crown be won.
   Of Mary, heaven's Queen and Gate,
   Devoted son was he,
   Who cherished all the ancient rites
   With great humility.

3. Fierce lover of the lowly life,
   True father of the poor,
   As you have done, so help us all
   To struggle and endure,
   That Christ be praised in ev'ry life,
   That riches not ensnare
   Or rule us in our daily walk;
   That strong may be our prayer!

J. MICHAEL THOMPSON
CMD, TUNE: "RESIGNATION" ("MY SHEPHERD WILL SUPPLY MY NEED")
TEXT COPYRIGHT 2010 WORLD LIBRARY PUBLICATIONS. USED WITH PERMISSION.

A Hymn for Saint Sharbel Makhluf

RESIGNATION
CMD

1. The moun - tain heights of Leb - a -
2. This monk and her - mit of the
3. Fierce lov - er of the low - ly

non Re - sound with songs of joy;
hills, Saint Mar - on's mod - est son,
life, True fath - er of the poor,

The ce - dars of that an - cient
Scorned wealth and com - fort in his
As you have done, so help us

land Stand tall as we em - ploy
life That heav - en's crown be won.
all To strug - gle and en - dure,

Our hymns of praise and thank - ful -
Of Mar - y, heav - en's Queen and
That Christ be praised in ev - 'ry

ness For Shar - bel's saint - ly ways,
Gate, De - vo - ted son was he,
life, That rich - es not en - snare

Lived out in strict hu - mil - i -
Who cher - ished all the an - cient
Or rule us in our dai - ly

ty That guid - ed all his days.
rites With great hu - mil - i - ty.
walk; That strong may be our prayer.

Patron of those who share in eucharistic adoration

SAINT
PETER JULIAN EYMARD
PRAY FOR US

FEAST
August 2
Born
February 4, 1811,
La Mure, France

DIED
August 1, 1868

CANONIZED
December 9, 1962,
by Pope John XXIII

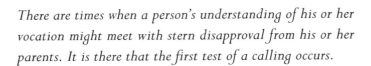

There are times when a person's understanding of his or her vocation might meet with stern disapproval from his or her parents. It is there that the first test of a calling occurs.

Peter Julian Eymard was born in a small town in southeastern France in 1811. His family was poor, and Peter worked with his father, a knife sharpener, until his eighteenth birthday.

In his spare time, he taught himself Latin and kept up with his studies enough that he was admitted to the seminary in the diocese of Grenoble. Here again, he met with disappointment, because he became seriously ill and was sent home to die.

God restored him to health, and in 1834 he was ordained a priest for the Grenoble diocese. In 1839, he received permission from his bishop to join the new Marist Congregation, where he worked hard and helped the young congregation grow. During this time, he struggled with the bad influence of the Jansenist heresy that believed only a certain number of people were predestined to be saved. This anxiety afflicted him with a strong striving for inner perfection, yet his great love for the Blessed Sacrament freed him from this scrupulous guilt of not being good enough to be one with God in heaven.

In 1856, Peter Julian received permission from his superiors to form a new congregation of priests, the Congregation of the Blessed Sacrament. This, like most new religious families in the Church, was fraught with poverty and suspicion from Church authorities. Nonetheless, his parish work in preparing children and adults for their first Communion, as well as his efforts to bring non-practicing Catholics back to the reception of the sacraments, bore remarkable fruit. At first, Peter sought to offer amends to the Lord for the indifference of Catholics to the Eucharist, but eventually he came to a spirituality of Christ-centered love. His men's community service was balanced between an active life of apostolic work and a contemplative life of adoration of Jesus in the Blessed Sacrament. He also worked with Marguerite Guillot to found the women's Congregation of the Servants of the Blessed Sacrament. He died in 1868.

[Jesus said,] "I am the true vine, and my Father is the vine grower. He takes away every branch in me that does not bear fruit, and everyone that does he prunes so that it bears more fruit. You are already pruned because of the word that I spoke to you. Remain in me, as I remain in you. Just as a branch cannot bear fruit on its own unless it remains on the vine, so neither can you unless you remain in me....By this is my Father glorified, that you bear much fruit and become my disciples."

JOHN 15:1–4, 8

"The Eucharist is the life of the people. The Eucharist gives them a center of life. All can come together without the barriers of race or language in order to celebrate the feast days of the Church. It gives them a law of life, that of charity, of which it is the source; thus it forges between them a common bond, a Christian kinship."

SAINT PETER JULIAN EYMARD

FOR REFLECTION

One of the greatest challenges in anyone's walk with the Lord is the ability to grow and change. Saint Peter Julian experienced several major changes in his spirituality as he strove to serve the Lord and the people of God. Today is a good day to reflect on our walk with the Lord and to see if we are listening to our own desires or to Christ.

PRAYER

O God,
you gave your Son Jesus Christ
to be the bread of life for your people.
Saint Peter Julian Eymard spent his life preaching and
    teaching
about this mystery of love and presence in the Church.

Give us grace to participate fruitfully in the Eucharist,
to cherish it and never take it for granted,
and to be eager to lead men and women to the sacred banquet.

We ask this through Christ our Lord.

Amen.

A Hymn for Saint Peter Julian Eymard

1. Lo! Angel's bread for food is giv'n
   To mortals here below;
   That ev'ry hungry heart be fed,
   And Christ's love might be known.
   Saint Peter Julian lived his life
   That all might love the Lord,
   That in the Blessed Sacrament
   Christ be fore'er adored.

2. He cried, his heart ablaze for Christ,
   "Tomorrow is too late!"
   Despite poor health and troubled times,
   He did not hesitate
   To found a group of priests to spread
   His zeal for Christ our Bread.
   He formed their lives with selfless zeal;
   They followed where he led.

3. To come to Christ's own heavn'ly feast
   Saint Peter gave his care
   To teach both children and adults
   With minds and hearts aware.
   Through years of scorn and poverty,
   Through toil and years of pain,
   He preached the love of Jesus Christ,
   Then heaven was his gain.

J. MICHAEL THOMPSON
CMD, TUNE: CAROL ("IT CAME UPON A MIDNIGHT CLEAR")
TEXT COPYRIGHT 2010 WORLD LIBRARY PUBLICATIONS. USED WITH PERMISSION.

A Hymn for Saint Peter Julian Eymard

CAROL
CMD

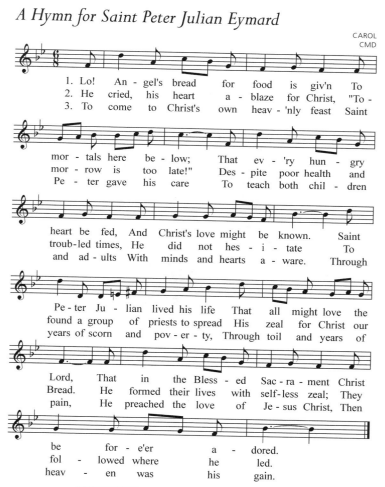

1. Lo! An - gel's bread for food is giv'n To mor - tals here be - low; That ev - 'ry hun - gry heart be fed, And Christ's love might be known. Saint Peter Ju - lian lived his life That all might love the Lord, That in the Bless - ed Sac - ra - ment Christ be for - e'er a - dored.

2. He cried, his heart a - blaze for Christ, "To - mor - row is too late!" Des - pite poor health and troub-led times, He did not hes - i - tate To found a group of priests to spread His zeal for Christ our Bread. He formed their lives with self-less zeal; They fol - lowed where he led.

3. To come to Christ's own heav - 'nly feast Saint Pe - ter gave his care To teach both chil - dren and ad - ults With minds and hearts a - ware. Through years of scorn and pov - er - ty, Through toil and years of pain, He preached the love of Je - sus Christ, Then heav - en was his gain.

Co-patron of Europe

SAINT
TERESA BENEDICTA
OF THE CROSS
(EDITH STEIN)

PRAY FOR US

FEAST

August 9

BORN

October 12, 1891,
Breslau, Dolnoslaskie, Germany
(now Wroclaw, Poland)

DIED

August 9, 1942,
in the gas chambers of Auschwitz,
Malopolskie (Poland)

CANONIZED

October 11, 1998,
by Pope John Paul II

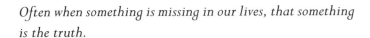

Often when something is missing in our lives, that something is the truth.

E dith Stein was born in 1891, on Yom Kippur, the Day of Atonement, as the youngest of eleven children in a Jewish family in Breslau, Germany. Her father died when she was two, and she was brought up by a devout and very strong mother. Edith did not remain an observer of the commandments, however. She went off to universities, starting in Breslau in 1911 and transferring to Goettingen in 1913. There she encountered the philosophy of "phenomenology" and Dr. Edmund Husserl. She graduated "with distinction" in 1915.

In the midst of her university experience, she became a nurse and cared for the sick during World War I. After this, she followed Husserl to the University of Freiburg, where she passed her doctorate *summa cum laude*, writing her dissertation on "The Problem of Empathy" in 1917.

Between 1917 and 1922, Edith realized she was searching for something missing inside herself. While she was reading a biography of Saint Teresa of Ávila, she said to herself, "This is the truth," and took up the faith. On January 1, 1922, Edith was baptized on the feast of the Circumcision of Jesus, now known as the feast of the Holy Name of Jesus. She said of herself, "I had given up practicing my Jewish faith when I was fourteen and did not begin to feel Jewish again until I had returned to God."

While she wanted to enter a Carmelite monastery immediately, her spiritual directors dissuaded her. They encouraged her to teach, to do public speaking, and to work toward reconciling philosophy with Catholic teaching. This effort led her to lecturing at the German Institute for Educational Studies at the University of Muenster. There she was able to combine scholarship and faith in her academic work. She said, "If anyone comes to me, I want to lead them to God."

With the rise of Adolf Hitler and his laws that were designed to show that the Jewish population was too large and drove Jews to concentration camps, it was impossible for Edith to continue teaching. She entered the Carmelite monastery in Cologne with the blessing of her spiritual father and after visiting her mother for the last time.

Edith Stein was invested in the Carmelite habit on April 15, 1934, and given the name Sister Teresa Benedicta of the Cross. Her mother died in Breslau on the day she took her vows. The holy card from her solemn profession contained the words of Saint John of the Cross: "Henceforth, my only vocation is to love."

Because of the horrors of the Nazi movement against the Jews of Germany, the prioress of the Carmel in Cologne arranged for Sister Teresa Benedicta to be smuggled across the German border into the Netherlands to the Carmel of Echt. Alas, the German army invaded and conquered the Netherlands and arrested Sister Teresa and her sister, Rosa, on August 2, 1942. After this arrest, the Roman Catholic bishops of the Netherlands wrote letters of protest against the pogroms and deportation of Jews from their country, as did many Christians of Jewish descent. Saint Teresa Benedicta was deported to Auschwitz along with 987 Jews, and she died in the gas chamber there, probably on August 9, just seven days after her arrival.

Then she prayed to the Lord, the God of Israel, saying: "My Lord, you alone are our King. Help me, who am alone and have no help but you, for I am taking my life in my hand."

ESTHER C:14–15

One can only gain a scientia cruicis *or knowledge of the cross, if he has thoroughly experienced the cross. I have been convinced of this from the first moment onwards and have said with all my heart, "*Ave Crux, spes unica!*" (Hail, Cross, our only hope!)*

FROM THE CARMELITE *LITURGY OF THE HOURS*
FOR HER FEAST

FOR REFLECTION

Today, faith and philosophy—indeed, faith and the academic world—are often seen as separate, not equal, if not irreconcilable. Sister Teresa Benedicta gave her life to the wedding of these two worlds. Let us keep our faith with us in all our endeavors as we work for the salvation of the world.

PRAYER

O God of Abraham,
your Son Jesus was circumcised,
lived under the Law,
and gave his life for the salvation of the whole world.

Through Saint Teresa Benedicta of the Cross' love for the
    cross of your Son
you brought the worlds of philosophy and theology into
    harmony.

Teach us the surrender to your will as she did,
even unto death, the ultimate victory.

We ask this through Jesus Christ, your Son, our Lord,
who lives and reigns with you and the Holy Spirit,
one God, forever and ever.

Amen.

A Hymn for Saint Teresa Benedicta of the Cross

1. O God of ancient Israel,
   Whose mercies never cease,
   Receive from us our song of praise,
   Our lasting hymn of peace.
   In midst of war and hateful acts,
   Despair and bitter strife,
   Your servant, Edith, served you well
   And won the crown of life.

2. She gained her knowledge of the Cross
   Through scholarship and pray'r,
   Which brought her closer to the Lord,
   The truth supreme and fair.
   From college walls to Carmel's cells
   You led her in your light,
   And kept her safe within your love
   Despite her soul's dark night.

3. O loving and sustaining God,
   O Triune, only Lord,
   O Father, Son, and Spirit blest,
   Your name be e'er adored!
   Your people have assembled
   To sing this martyr's praise:
   Grace us to love you faithfully,
   And serve you all our days.

J. MICHAEL THOMPSON
CMD, TUNE: "FOREST GREEN"
TEXT COPYRIGHT 2010 WORLD LIBRARY PUBLICATIONS. USED WITH PERMISSION.

A Hymn for Saint Teresa Benedicta of the Cross

FOREST GREEN
CMD

1. O God of an-cient Is-ra-el, Whose mer-cies nev-er cease, Re-ceive from us our song of praise, Our last-ing hymn of peace. In midst of war and hate-ful acts, Des-pair and bit-ter strife, Your ser-vant E-dith served you well And won the crown of life.

2. She gained her know-ledge of the Cross Through scho-lar-ship and pray'r, Which brought her clo-ser to the Lord, The truth su-preme and fair. From col-lege walls to Car-mel's cells You led her in your light, And kept her safe with-in your love Des-pite her soul's dark night.

3. O lov-ing and sus-tain-ing God, O Tri-une, on-ly Lord, O Fath-er, Son and Spir-it blest, Your name be e'er a-dored! Your peo-ple have as-sem-bled here To sing this mar-tyr's praise: Grace us to love you faith-ful-ly, And serve you all our days.

TEXT COPYRIGHT 2010 WORLD LIBRARY PUBLICATIONS. USED WITH PERMISSION

Patron of civil defense volunteers
and Catholic adolescents

SAINT PIO OF PIETRELCINA

PRAY FOR US

FEAST

September 23

BORN

May 25, 1887,
Pietrelcina, Benevento, Italy

DIED

September 23, 1968,
San Giovanni Rotondo, Foggia, Italy

CANONIZED

June 16, 2002,
by Pope John Paul II

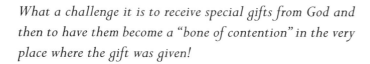

What a challenge it is to receive special gifts from God and then to have them become a "bone of contention" in the very place where the gift was given!

F rancisco Forgione was born to a farming family in southern Italy in 1887. When he was fifteen, he joined the Capuchin Franciscans and took the name of Pio (Pius). In 1910, after the normal course of studies, he was ordained to the priesthood. Very soon after that, in 1914, World War I began, and Father Pio was drafted into the Italian army. He then discovered he had tuberculosis and was discharged. The friars sent him home to his family until his health could improve. In 1917, he was assigned to the Capuchin friary in San Giovanni Rotondo, about seventy-five miles from Bari, Italy, on the Adriatic Sea.

In 1918, he was praying in thanksgiving after celebrating Mass when he had a vision of Jesus. After the vision ended, Father Pio had the stigmata or wounds of the Lord Jesus in his hands, feet, and side. This led to a time of severe trial, since medical doctors questioned the authenticity of the stigmata. Father Pio was no longer allowed to celebrate Mass in public or to hear confessions. Although this was difficult for him, Pio did not complain, and eventually these restrictions were lifted.

After receiving the stigmata, Pio rarely left his friary. However, busloads of pilgrims came to see him. He would preside at Mass around 5 a.m. and then hear confessions until noon. Eventually he would hear confessions for ten hours every day. Saint Pio was also well-known for his devotion to the sick and the suffering.

He did not, however, make prophecies, as some people falsely claimed, and he did not make statements on things he felt were only to be decided by proper Church authorities. He often was quoted as saying, "I only want to be a friar who prays." He lived and died under obedience to his superiors, and passed from death to life on September 23, 1968.

Although you have not seen him you love him; even though you do not see him now yet believe in him, you rejoice with an indescribable and glorious joy.

1 PETER 1:8

*"Through the study of books,
one seeks God. Through meditation,
one finds him."*

SAINT PIO

FOR REFLECTION

Saint Pio, you are widely known for a special gift from God that allowed you to see Jesus and, thereafter, to actually experience the same wounds as those that our Lord suffered. Ironically, this gift caused consternation among people who did not believe this happened to you. Yet you did not let that negativity interfere with your deep-seeded desire and ability to pray for others, especially those who were ill. Help us, Saint Pio, to refrain from discouragement when others question our own special gifts. As the friar who only wanted to pray, we know we can depend on you to be at our side when discouragement gets in our way.

PRAYER

O loving God,
you sent your Son, Jesus Christ, into the world
that, through his suffering and death,
we might be freed from sin and born again in grace.

Following the example of your servant, Saint Pio,
let us truly understand that,
"To live is Christ, and to die is gain."

Give us strength to treasure your gifts,
even when others deny their grace.

Help us to love you always in the poor,
the sick and the needy.
We ask this through Christ our Lord.

Amen.

A Hymn for Saint Padre Pio

1. The God who calls the least of all
   To follow and obey,
   In poverty and chastity
   Saint Francis' lesser way.

2. Today has raised a simple priest,
   From common peasant place,
   And made of him a confidant
   Of heav'n's amazing grace.

3. Saint Pio, lover of the One
   Who gave himself as bread,
   Showed forth this love to penitents
   Whose souls in Christ he fed.

J. MICHAEL THOMPSON
CM, "NEW BRITAIN" ("AMAZING GRACE")
TEXT COPYRIGHT 2010 WORLD LIBRARY PUBLICATIONS. USED WITH PERMISSION.

A Hymn for Saint Padre Pio

NEW BRITAIN
CM

1. The God who calls the least of
2. To - day has raised a sim - ple
3. Saint Pi - o, lov - er of the

all To fol - low and o - bey,
priest, From com - mon peas - ant place,
One Who gave him - self as bread,

In pov - er - ty and chas - ti -
And made of him a con - fi -
Showed forth this love to pen - i -

ty Saint Fran - cis' less - er way,
dant Of heav'n's a - maz - ing grace.
tents Whose souls in Christ he fed.

Patron of Filipino youth, people living in poverty, altar servers, and catechists

SAINT
LORENZO RUIZ
& COMPANIONS
PRAY FOR US

FEAST
September 28

BORN
c.1600,
at Binondo,
Manila, Philippines

DIED
September 1637,
Nagasaki, Japan

CANONIZED
October 18, 1987,
by Pope John Paul II

Have you ever taken a trip that you thought *would take you to one destination but instead took you in another direction altogether? That's what happened to Saint Lorenzo (Lawrence) Ruiz.*

Saint Lorenzo was born in Manila to a Chinese father and a Filipina mother around 1600. Lorenzo participated in the Church from a very young age. He studied with Dominican friars, who taught him Spanish and calligraphy. This permitted him to become a professional calligrapher. He married and had two sons and a daughter.

Then, sometime in 1636, Lorenzo was suspected of being involved in a serious crime. He learned that a ship was leaving Manila with some Dominican missionaries. Believing that the boat was headed for the Portuguese colony of Macao, he received permission to leave with them. Only once the ship had set sail did Lorenzo find out that it was headed to Japan, where Christians were suffering a terrible persecution.

No sooner had the boat landed on Okinawa than the Japanese authorities arrested all of the Christians aboard and took them to Nagasaki. There, Lorenzo and his companions were all subjected to horrible torture, which lasted for several days. Lorenzo died there, he was cremated by the authorities, and his ashes were thrown into the sea.

In 1981, Blessed John Paul II beatified Saint Lorenzo and his companions on a papal visit to Manila, and canonized them in Rome in 1987. Saint Lorenzo Ruiz is the first person from the Philippines to be canonized and is also the first person from there to be martyred.

But even if you should suffer because of righteousness, blessed are you. Do not be afraid or terrified with fear of them, but sanctify Christ as Lord in your hearts. Always be ready to give an explanation to anyone who asks you for a reason for your hope.

1 PETER 3:14–15

When asked by his torturer if he would abandon the faith to save his life, Saint Lorenzo responded: "That I shall never do, because I am a Christian—and I shall die for God, and for him I will give many thousands of lives if I had them. So do with me as you please."

FOR REFLECTION

As a young man, Saint Lorenzo was famous for his calligraphy, as he took words and put them down on paper with ink and color and gold leaf to create works of beauty out of everyday messages. Our life can do the same as we perform ordinary acts of love, even when they don't seem to be of great consequence. God sees.

PRAYER

O God,
you sustain all your people
through the changes and chances of this life.

Thank you for the life and witness
of Saint Lorenzo Ruiz and his companions,
who refused to betray your Son,
and remained faithful despite suffering torture and death.

May their courage and zeal for the Gospel
illumine our dark days and nights,
that we, too, may follow Jesus Christ,
the Light of the World,
who lives and reigns with you and the Holy Spirit,
one God, now and forever.

Amen.

A Hymn for Saint Lorenzo Ruiz & Companions

1. Go forth, Christ said, proclaiming,
   Baptizing, as you teach
   My gospel to all people;
   And by your living, preach
   The way that I have shown you—
   Not hidden or sublime—
   And know that I am with you
   Beyond the end of time.

2 When taken into prison
   And told he could be freed
   If only he'd deny you
   And others with him lead,
   He told his faith more boldly,
   Full-voiced and bright of eye;
   They killed him and his workmates,
   Who chose for you to die.

3. For men like good Saint Lawrence,
   We give you thanks and praise.
   As catechist he served you
   Through endless journey days,
   From Philippines, his homeland,
   To shores of far Japan,
   He told your love and mercy,
   In spite of rulers' ban.

J. MICHAEL THOMPSON
76 76 D, TUNE: "PASSION CHORALE" ("O SACRED HEAD SURROUNDED")
TEXT COPYRIGHT 2010 WORLD LIBRARY PUBLICATIONS. USED WITH PERMISSION.

A Hymn for Saint Lorenzo Ruiz & Companions

PASSION CHORALE
76 76 D

1. Go forth, Christ said, pro - claim - ing, Bap -
2. When ta - ken in - to pris - on And
3. For men like good Saint Law - rence, We

tiz - ing, as you teach My gos - pel to all
told he could be freed If on - ly he'd de -
give you thanks and praise. As cat - e - chist he

peo - ple; And by your liv - ing, preach The
ny you And oth - ers with him lead, He
served you Through end - less jour - ney days, From

way that I have shown you— Not hid - den or sub -
told his faith more bold - ly, Full - voiced and bright of
Phil - ip - pines, his home - land, To shores of far Jap -

lime— And know that I am with you Be -
eye; They killed him and his work - mates, Who
an, He told your love and mer - cy, In

yond the end of time.
chose for you to die.
spite of ru - lers' ban.

Patron of parish priests in Vietnam

SAINT
ANDREW DUNG-LAC
& COMPANIONS
PRAY FOR US

FEAST
November 24

BORN
1795,
Vietnam

DIED
December 21, 1839,
Vietnam

CANONIZED
June 19, 1988,
by Pope John Paul II

The only association many citizens of the United States have with Vietnam is that it is a country where the United States lost a war. There is rarely any thought given to the fact that many Vietnamese citizens are members of the Catholic Church, or that they live in a country where being a Catholic can mean persecution and even imprisonment.

Saint Andrew Dung-Lac and his 117 companions stand in witness to the words of the early Church Father, Tertullian: "The blood of the martyrs is the seed of the Church." This collection of "white-robed army of martyrs" was gathered into heaven between 1820 and 1862. They included priests, religious, and laypersons, both Vietnamese-born and European missionaries.

The saint whose name is at the head of this list was Andrew Dung-Lac, a man born to a poor family in 1795 in the northern part of what is today Vietnam. When his family moved into the capital city of Hanoi, he met a Catholic catechist who gave him shelter and instruction in the faith. He took the name Andrew when he was baptized. After learning both Chinese and Latin and being mentored through his theological studies, he was ordained to the priesthood in 1823. He ministered to a parish where his simple and strictly ascetic life brought about many conversions to the Catholic faith. He was arrested for being a Christian three different times during the persecution of the Emperor Minh-Mang. The third time, in 1839, he was tortured and beheaded.

The Martyrs of Vietnam are just one of the "martyr groups" commemorated on the General Roman Calendar. Others include the Martyrs of Uganda (June 3), the Martyrs of China (July 9), the Martyrs of Japan (Feb. 6), and the First Martyrs of the Church of Rome (June 30). Pope John Paul II canonized Saint Andrew in 1988.

...We boast in hope of the glory of God.

ROMANS 5:2

"Let nothing else be now in your hearts and minds except God's commandments and the precepts of heaven....Let no one think of death, but only of immortality; let no one think of suffering that is for a time, but only of glory that is for eternity."

FROM A LETTER BY SAINT CYPRIAN OF CARTHAGE, BISHOP AND MARTYR, FROM *LITURGY OF THE HOURS*

FOR REFLECTION

The last time that Saint Andrew Dung-Lac was arrested, it was because he went to visit a fellow priest, Saint Peter Thi, to go to confession. He went to receive the sacrament, even though he knew he was risking his life. How much do we treasure and practice the sacrament of reconciliation? Would you give your life to be forgiven, reconciled to God and the Church?

PRAYER

Loving God,
you have surrounded us, your faithful people,
with a great cloud of witnesses,
whose devotion to you was sealed in their death.

May the testimony of Saint Andrew Dung-Lac
and his many companions give us courage
to face the daily challenges we experience.

We ask this through Jesus Christ our Lord.

Amen.

A Hymn for Saint Andrew Dung Lac & Companions

1. "Fear not those who kill the body;
   Rather those who steal the soul;
   On your head, each hair is numbered.
   God himself will keep you whole."

2. We give thanks for Andrew Dung-Lac,
   Faithful priest, and for his friends,
   Raised by God to preach and nurture
   Vietnam to Christian ends.

3. When the days of persecution
   Overtook the Church, they stood
   Firm in faith against oppression,
   Boasting in the cross's good.

J. MICHAEL THOMPSON
87 87, TUNE: "STUTTGART" ("COME, O LONG-EXPECTED JESUS")
TEXT COPYRIGHT 2010 WORLD LIBRARY PUBLICATIONS. USED WITH PERMISSION.

A Hymn for Saint Andrew Dung Lac & Companions

STUTTGART
87 87

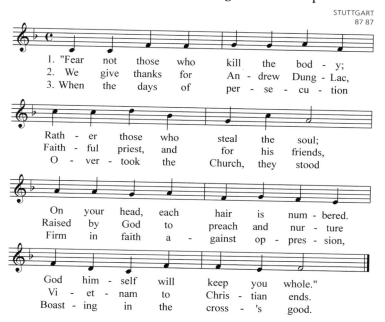

1. "Fear not those who kill the bod - y;
2. We give thanks for An - drew Dung - Lac,
3. When the days of per - se - cu - tion

Rath - er those who steal the soul;
Faith - ful priest, and for his friends,
O - ver - took the Church, they stood

On your head, each hair is num - bered.
Raised by God to preach and nur - ture
Firm in faith a - gainst op - pres - sion,

God him - self will keep you whole."
Vi - et - nam to Chris - tian ends.
Boast - ing in the cross - 's good.

*Patron of unmarried girls, educators, girls, jurists,
lawyers, librarians, mechanics, millers, milliners,
hat-makers, nurses, secretaries, students, theologians*

SAINT CATHERINE OF ALEXANDRIA

PRAY FOR US

FEAST

November 25

BORN

c. 282,

Alexandria, Egypt

DIED

c. 310,

Alexandria, Egypt

CANONIZED

Before the official process began

The Roman Martyrology *of 2002 says, "Saint Catherine, about whom it is told that she was an Alexandrian and a martyr, filled with sharpness of mind and wisdom no less than with strength of soul. Her body is honored in pious veneration at the Monastery of Saint Catherine on Mount Sinai. She was martyred [around]* AD *310."*

We have very few facts about Saint Catherine of Alexandria, and that led the Roman Catholic Church to remove her from the General Roman Calendar of saints in 1969. She was, however, never removed from the great collection of saints called the *Roman Martyrology*, and in 2002 she was returned to the General Roman Calendar as an optional memorial.

Since her death, she has been revered as a "great martyr" by the Byzantine Churches, and their great regard for her is reflected in the Troparion sung for her feast:

"You enlightened the pagan philosophers with the light of your works. You were like a full moon for those who travel at night. You overcame the darkness and converted the queen. You stood up to the torturer, O blessed Catherine, chosen by God. On your wishes you were carried to the heavenly bridal chamber of your splendid Bridegroom, Christ You were espoused to him with a regal crown, O bride chosen by God. In the company of the angels, pray for us who keep your memory."

So, the Christians of the Eastern and Western Churches keep festivals for Saint Catherine and hold her up as a model of faithfulness to our Lord Jesus Christ, even to the point of suffering and death—and commemorate her as well for mental fidelity to the Word of God, beyond all earthly philosophies.

Rather, we speak God's wisdom, mysterious, hidden, which God predetermined before the ages for our glory.

1 CORINTHIANS 2:7

O lovers of the martyrs, let us joyfully gather together
for the feast of the God-wise martyr Catherine. Let us
cover her with praises as though with flowers. Let us
cry out to her: Rejoice! since her teaching confounded
the erring orators. They were full of ignorance, and she
tutored them in the divine faith. Rejoice, O dedicated
handmaiden! Your body was given over to many
torturers, because of your love for the Creator of All.
We extol you, since you have inherited heaven as the
reward for your earthly pains. Now you are delighting
in eternal light. We sing a hymn to you and hope
to share in your glory!

FROM THE VESPERS FOR SAINT CATHERINE
OF ALEXANDRIA, BYZANTINE CHURCH

FOR REFLECTION

Saint Catherine of Alexandria lived in an age where competing philosophies pulled at minds and hearts. However, she pointed us to the words of the Apostle Paul, "I say this to you so that no one may deceive you by specious arguments...so, as you received Christ Jesus the Lord, walk in him, rooted in him and built upon him and established in the faith as you were taught, abounding in thanksgiving. See to it that no one captivate you with an empty, seductive philosophy according to human tradition...and not according to Christ" (Colossians 2:4, 6–8).

PRAYER

O God,
source of all true wisdom,
we give you thanks today for the steadfast witness of
	your martyr,
Catherine of Alexandria.

Give us, we ask you,
the same faithfulness to our Lord and Savior Jesus Christ
that she showed when she was challenged by other
	philosophies,
even to the offering up of her very life as a living sacrifice.

Help us witness to your truth with love and strength.
We ask this through Christ our Lord.

Amen.

A Hymn for Saint Catherine of Alexandria

1. Raise, O saints, the strains of glory
   For this martyred woman's fame.
   Let us venerate the wisdom
   Which is sung of Catherine's name!
   From the pulpit of a furnace
   She preached Christ, her Lord and King,
   Silencing the pagan wise men.
   Hymns of praise now let us sing!

2. Crowned by Christ in mystic marriage,
   Undefeated in the strife
   Forced on her by evildoers,
   She passed through from death to life.
   Like the moon for nighttime travel,
   She reflects the throne of grace,
   And, with countless saints and angels,
   Stands before the Lord's own face.

3. Glory now to God the Father
   Who has made us for his own;
   Glory now to Christ our Savior,
   Seated on the judgment throne;
   Glory now to God the Spirit,
   Source of love and font of grace;
   With the martyrs, all the ransomed
   Sing this song through time and space!

J. MICHAEL THOMPSON
87 87 D, TUNE: "HYFRYDOL" ("ALLELUIA! SING TO JESUS")
TEXT COPYRIGHT 2010 WORLD LIBRARY PUBLICATIONS. USED WITH PERMISSION.

A Hymn for Saint Catherine of Alexandria

HYFRYDOL
87 87 D

1. Raise, O saints, the strains of glo - ry
2. Crowned by Christ in mys - tic mar - riage,
3. Glo - ry now to God the Fath - er

For this mar - tyred wo - man's fame.
Un - de - feat - ed in the strife
Who has made us for his own;

Let us ven - er - ate the wis - dom
Forced on her by e - vil - do - ers,
Glo - ry now to Christ our Sav - ior,

Which is sung of Cath - erine's name!
She passed through from death to life.
Seat - ed on the judg - ment throne;

From the pul - pit of a fur - nace
Like the moon for night - time trav - el,
Glo - ry now to God the Spir - it.

She preached Christ, her Lord and King.
She re - flects the throne of grace,
Source of love and font of grace;

Si - lenc - ing the pa - gan wise - men.
And, with count - less saints and an - gels,
With the mar - tyrs, all the ran - somed

Hymns of praise now let us sing!
Stands be - fore the Lord's own face.
Sing this song through time and space!

FEAST DAY, SAINT, AND
MEMORIAL REQUIREMENT

JANUARY 6 — *André Bessette, optional memorial in the U.S.*

FEBRUARY 8 — *Josephine Bakhita, optional memorial*

APRIL 23 — *Adalbert, optional memorial*

APRIL 28 — *Louis Mary de Monfort, optional memorial*

MAY 10 — *Damien of Molokai, optional memorial in the U.S.*

MAY 21 — *Christopher Magallanes and companions, optional memorial*

MAY 22 — *Rita of Cascia, optional memorial*

JULY 9 — *Augustine Zhao Rong and companions, optional memorial*

JULY 20 — *Apollinaris, optional memorial*

JULY 24 — *Sharbel Makhluf, optional memorial*

AUGUST 2 — *Peter Julian Eymard, optional memorial*

AUGUST 9 — *Teresa Benedicta of the Cross, optional memorial*

SEPTEMBER 23 — *Pio of Pietrelcina, memorial*

SEPTEMBER 28 — *Lorenzo (Lawrence) Ruiz and companions, optional memorial*

NOVEMBER 24 — *Andrew Dung-Lac and companions, memorial*

NOVEMBER 25 — *Catherine of Alexandria, optional memorial*